Euripides

Iphigenia at Aulis

Translation by David Bolton

Published by Lulu Books

2019

Copyright by David Bolton

ISBN 978-0-244-22455-4

Terms for the performance of this play may be obtained from
David Bolton at dgbolton0@gmail.com.

All translations in this edition, including the introductory sections (unless specifically attributed) are by David Bolton.

Colour: #004126

Contents

The background to *Iphigenia at Aulis*   6

The original production of the play   9

The central characters   9

Rhetoric in Iphigenia at Aulis   12

Aulis   13

Origins and Life of Euripides   14

Structure of *Iphigenia at Aulis*   20

Iphigenia at Aulis   21

Dramatis personae   22

Iphigenia at Aulis   23

The background to *Iphigenia at Aulis*
The setting of *Iphigenia at Aulis* is the assembly of the Greek fleet at Aulis, ready to depart for Troy under the command of Agamemnon. But the Goddess Artemis has been offended and prevents the fleet from setting sail: she demands, through the medium of the priest Calchas, the ritual sacrifice of Iphigenia, Agamemnon's daughter. Agamemnon is the most powerful king in Greece and leads the expedition. But, the expedition is for the benefit of Menelaüs, whose wife Helen has been seduced, abducted and taken to Troy by Paris. It is Agamemnon's daughter whose sacrifice is demanded, and Agamemnon has summoned Iphigenia to Aulis, accompanied by her mother, Clytemnestra, on the pretext of marrying the great warrior, Achilles.

The earliest known mention of Iphigenia's story is in the *Cypria*, a lost epic poem attributed to Stasinus, a poet of the late eighth century BC. This poem about the Trojan Wars related how the Greeks under Agamemnon gathered at Aulis (for a second time after a failed first excursion) and that the divination of the priest Calchas led to Iphigenia's being brought to Aulis to be sacrificed to the Goddess Artemis; and that the goddess saved Iphigenia at the last moment, taking her to the land of the Taurians and substituting a deer to be sacrificed in her stead.

Homer, however, makes no mention of Iphigenia or her story. Agamemnon, the leader of the Greek expedition, and Achilles, the greatest of the Greek warriors, are central characters of the *Iliad*, a poem which begins with a dispute between Agamemnon and Achilles over a slave girl and concludes with Achilles' victory over the Trojan hero, Hector. Menelaüs plays a prominent part: indeed the Trojan War is being fought over his wife, Helen. Clytemnestra is mentioned in the *Odyssey*, where a comparison arises on the one hand, between Agamemnon, his son Orestes, and Aegisthus (who takes control of Mycenae along with Clytemnestra) and on the other, Odysseus, his son Telemachus and the suitors (who try to take over Odysseus' home of Ithaca and Penelope, Odysseus' wife). Clytemnestra's subsequent murder of

Agamemnon on his return from Troy is also recounted in the *Odyssey*. In this account, Clytemnestra is regarded as the villain, who, in Agamemnon's absence in Troy, set up home in Mycenae with Aegisthus. On Agamemnon's return from the war, she and Aegisthus murdered him. He had not helped his cause by returning to Mycenae in the company of the Trojan princess, Cassandra, as his concubine, whom Clytemnestra also kills. Aegisthus and, it is implied, Clytemnestra are in turn murdered by Orestes, who returned from Athens in the eighth year after Agamemnon's murder to carry out the deed.

Orestes makes his appearance as a baby in *Iphigenia at Aulis*. There arose a tradition, again not in Homer, but recounted in Aeschylus' *Oresteia* trilogy, that Orestes, having murdered his mother, was pursued by the Furies, avenging deities born of Gaia (Earth) and the blood of Ouranos (the Sky). The issue of matricide was settled with Orestes' eventual acquittal on such a charge at the Athenian court of the Areopagus.

In *Iphigenia at Aulis*, Iphigenia, at the moment of sacrifice, simply disappears. Euripides continues her story, however, in *Iphigenia amongst the Taurians*. In this account, which follows broadly the story set out by Stasinus in the *Cypria*, the goddess had taken Iphigenia from the place of sacrifice to her temple situated in the land of the Taurians, in the region of what is now Sevastopol in the Crimea. Iphigenia continues her life serving Artemis as her priestess. After several years, Orestes, in spite of being acquitted at the court of the Areopagus, is still being pursued by some of the Furies, who had refused to be appeased. He had sought the advice of Apollo, who had told him to go to the land of the Taurians in order to bring the image of Artemis from her temple there to Athens. On reaching the temple, he recognized the priestess of the temple to be Iphigenia. On the intervention of the goddess Athene, the story is brought to a satisfactory conclusion. Orestes brought both Iphigenia and the image of Artemis back to Athens. The image was established in a temple dedicated to Artemis at Brauron, a few mile outside Athens. Iphigenia became the priestess of the temple. Athene says to her: "Your particular care will be childbirth and when you die, you shall be buried there and your memorial will be made of finely woven cloth left from women who have died in labour".

The story of Iphigenia seems to have been known by the Taurians themselves. Herodotus, the fifth century historian, tells us:
"The Taurians have the following customs: they sacrifice to the virgin goddess the seafarers and any Greeks whom they capture. The sacrifice is made as follows: Having begun the ceremonies, they beat the victim's head with a club. Some say they push the body over the cliff (the temple is built on the top of the cliff) and put the head on a stake. Others agree about the head, but say the body is not pushed over the cliff but buried in the earth. The virgin goddess is identified by the Taurians themselves as Iphigenia, the daughter of Agamemnon." *[Herodotus, Histories 4.103]*

The remains of a fifth century temple dedicated to Artemis still exist at Brauron. There is archaeological evidence of worship at the site from at least the eighth century.

However, various other sites in Greece claim to have been the recipient of the image of Artemis and to have been associated with Iphigenia. Pausanias, writing in the second century AD, says in a description of Sparta:
"The place called 'The Marshes' is sacred to Artemis the Standing. The wooden image there, they say is the one that Orestes and Iphigenia stole from the land of the Taurians. The Spartans say it was brought to their land since Orestes was also king there. Their account seems to me more likely than that of the Athenians. For what reason would Iphigenia leave the image at Brauron? And why, when the Athenians were preparing to abandon their land, did they not think to put it also on board their ships? And yet the name of the Goddess of the Taurians has endured to the present day: so much so that the Capadocians living on the shores of the Euxine Sea *[Black Sea]* claim that the image is with them; and a similar claim is made by the Lydians who have

the Temple of Artemis Anaeitis. Yet the Athenians thought little of it when it was seized by the Persians: it was taken from Brauon to Susa, and later, Seleucus gave it to the Syrians of Laodicea, who have it to this day." *[Pausanias, Description of Greece 3.17.7]*

The original production of the play

Euripides is thought to have commenced writing this play whilst living in Macedon towards the end of his life, but to have died (in 406 BC) before completing it. The play is said to have been produced after Euripides' death by another Euripides, the tragedian's son or nephew. The play had, by then, been completed by other hands. There has been considerable discussion since the early eighteenth century as to which sections of the play are by Euripides himself and which sections represent the work of later writers.

The central characters

The play and its central characters are open to considerable interpretation. A key issue about many of the central characters is that of change – change of stance taken, or change in character as a whole – as the play progresses.

Agamemnon changes his view more than once as to whether Iphigenia should be summoned to Aulis at all. He does not appear to relish deceit or to be a man of indifference. After her sacrifice, however, he makes only a brief and unapologetic appearance and is presumed to be engaged in organizing the putting to sea of his fleet; and so, after the event, he shows no remorse or contrition nor does he attempt to comfort Clytemnestra. Has he simply sacrificed his daughter to pursue his own ambitions? Or do we give him at least partially the benefit of the doubt and conclude that he is an indecisive man out of his depth?

Menelaüs, a Spartan, is rarely a sympathetic character in Athenian tragedy. Firstly, in this play, he goads Agamemnon to continue with the sacrifice and then, when successful, he retracts his demand. Is this a genuine change of heart? Does he cleverly realise the sacrifice is inevitable? Or is he, perhaps like Agamemnon, simply indecisive?

Achilles' character undergoes change in its developing admiration of Iphigenia. He begins by being disdainful of Agamemnon's plan of deceit:
"I would be the lowest of the Greek soldiers here... if my name were put to your husband's slaughtering his daughter."
However, he clarifies his position:
"...he should have asked for the use of my name as bait. ... I would have allowed it, if our journey to Troy depended on it. I would not refuse to help the common good of those with whom I campaign."
In other words, Achilles objection is not the deceit itself but the perceived insult to himself of using his name without his permission.
But when Iphigenia insists that she be sacrificed for the benefit of the Greek nations, Achilles' views change. He admires her, wants her as his wife and is prepared to take on all the Greek armies more or less single-handedly in her defence:
"...some god would intend to make me happy indeed if I were to win your hand in marriage! I envy Greece for winning you, and I admire you for your love of Greece! ... See here: I would like to show kindness to you and take you to my home. And, by my mother Thetis, I shall grieve if I do not do battle with the Greeks and save you".

Clytemnestra, Iphigenia's mother, is a consistent character, but one which is affected by changing emotions: she enters as an almost overprotective mother, she shows interest as her husband tells her about her prospective son-in-law, she shows defiance when Agamemnon tells her she will not be present at the marriage ceremony, she is delighted when she first meets Achilles, she is horrified on learning of her daughter's impending fate, she clings to the hope that Achilles might save her, and she is left angry and distraught at the end of the play. She is portrayed, (as is not always the case in recounting her story) in a sympathetic light. However, the constant presence of the baby Orestes is of particular note. The audience of the day would have been aware of events unfolding much later: that after the war, Agamemnon returned to be murdered by Clytemnestra, and that Clytemnestra was, years later, murdered in turn by Orestes. There are numerous references to Fate and Necessity in the play. Just as Iphigenia heads helplessly towards her fate, so do Agamemnon and Clytemnestra as the cycle of bloodshed continues.

Iphigenia herself undergoes a considerable transition. She is introduced on her arrival at Aulis as a delicate young girl with her protective mother, and she is reduced to floods of tears on learning of her intended death. She quickly develops, however, into a heroine insisting on facing death for the sake of the honour of Greece.

Aristotle, in fact, criticized this depiction of Iphigenia:

"[a character should be] consistent. Even if the original person who is the basis of the character is inconsistent, nevertheless it must be consistently inconsistent…An example of an inconsistent character is Iphigenia at Aulis: when a suppliant, she is unlike her later self." *[Aristotle, Poetics 15]*

The theatregoer, however, may well be happy with the transition she undoubtedly undergoes: perhaps the delicate young girl simply has hidden depths. There are, though, other matters of interest. Iphigenia ultimately chooses death in the interests of Greece, even though Achilles had offered to defend her. She is presented as a heroine. But was her patriotism misguided? She identifies Greek interests with the recovery of Helen. But was the recovery of Menelaüs' wife a cause worth dying for? Perhaps we are simply expected to accept her heroism at face value. Or perhaps, with the gods against her and believing her own rhetoric, she was a tragic heroine who faced Necessity, just as Agamemnon, Clytemnestra and Orestes would face Necessity in their turn. As Achilles observed when commending her decision:

"You are right not to fight the gods, who are too strong for you, but to think of nobility and necessity".

11

Rhetoric in *Iphigenia at Aulis*

The Assembly of the people had been established in Athens in the early sixth century and had become the sovereign body by the mid fifth century. The aristocratic Pericles and the demagogue Cleon were amongst those who swayed the assembled Athenians with their oratory. Oratory mattered. Vital decisions were made by the Assembly in times of war, peace, empire and essential diplomacy; and the Assembly was persuaded by the oratory of its speakers.

At this time also, sophists set themselves up as teachers of 'virtue', a subject which encompassed not only moral rectitude, but more especially, a general ability to manage one's own and the state's affairs. A considerable portion of the sophists' teaching was concerned with rhetoric, and this in turn roused considerable interest in rhetoric amongst the Athenians.

There was also philosophical interest in the concept of virtue at this time. Clearly, rhetoric was relevant: rhetoric seeks to influence our judgment in relation to virtuous acts, to influence, in fact, what we consider virtuous in any given circumstance. The teacher and philosopher, Protagoras, held that 'Man is the measure of all things': that where judgments are concerned, we have to arrive at our own conclusions, but not to rely on either the gods or identifying absolute truth. Not everyone agreed. Plato, for his part, countered that there were absolute truths (the problem for mere humans was to perceive them) and that our knowledge of them helps us in the exercise of the 'art of measurement' required to determine how properly to act in a given situation.

The power of oratory was also recognized by the Athenian historian Thucydides. His historical narrative is interspersed with set speeches, as historical figures, at critical moments, state their case: an ambassador making his case before another state, Pericles' funeral speech delivered by his son, speeches before the Athenian Assembly, a general speaking to his army.

Rhetoric, so much a part of Athenian life, was reflected in the tragic plays. In *Iphigenia at Aulis*, the speeches of Agamemnon and Menelaüs in the First Episode are clearly rhetorical in character, as each man criticizes the other and argues persuasively for or against the sacrifice of Iphigenia. In the Conclusion,

Clytemnestra, Iphigenia and Agamemnon all speak oratorically to present the case for, or justification of, the stances they are taking. Only Achilles, the plain-speaking soldier, speaks clearly, but tries to persuade no-one.

But rhetoric, in the play, does not, it is felt, change the course of tragic events: as Achilles tells us, there is a futility in fighting against the gods and against the rule of Necessity.

Aulis

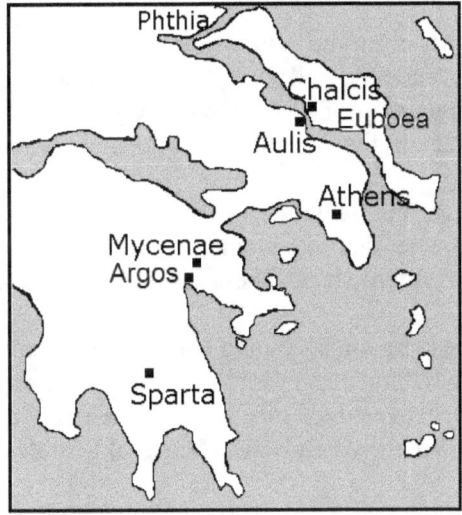

Aulis provides a large sheltered bay on the northern Greek mainland giving access to the narrow channel (the Euripus) between the mainland and the island of Euboea.

Origins and Life of Euripides

[A translation of the text of the 'Origins and Life of Euripides' is set out below. The original was transmitted along with the texts of Euripides plays, but its own origin is not known. It does not constitute a single account: sections Ia and III are considered to derive from related sources, section Ib appears to stand alone and repeats some of what is in Ia and III, and II and IV have elements from a different source.]

Ia. Euripides the poet was born the son of Mnesarchides[1], a shopkeeper, and Cleito a vegetable seller. He was an Athenian, born in Salamis, in the archonship of Calliades in the year of the 75th Olympiad[2], at the time of the Greek sea-battle against the Persians[3].

He trained, to begin with, for the pankration[4] or boxing, since his father had received an oracle that he would be victorious in contests where the winner is crowned. They say he did win a victory at Athens.

Having studied, he turned to tragedy and introduced many innovations[5]: enquiries into natural causes, rhetorical speeches and recognitions, as would be expected of one who was a pupil of Anaxagoras, Prodicus and Protagoras and was a friend of Socrates.

---

[1] Elsewhere referred to as Mnesarchus.

[2] 480BC.

[3] The battle of Salamis, as referred to below.

[4] Pancration: a combined form of wrestling and boxing.

[5] Different readings of the texts suggest an additional innovation may have been 'prologues'.

Both the philosopher Socrates and Mnesilochus seemed to have collaborated with him: as Telecleides says: "Mnesilochus proposes some fresh Phrygian drama for Euripides and so does Socrates." [1] Others say Cephisophon or the Argive Timocrates composed songs for him.

They say that he became a painter and that he showed his paintings in Megara; and that he became a torch-bearer of Apollo Zosterius; and that he was born on the same day as Hellanicus[2] on which the Greeks were victorious at the sea-battle of Salamis; and that he first entered the drama competitions when he was 26 years old.

He settled in Magnesia[3] and was honoured with privileges[4] and freedom from taxes.

From there he went to Macedonia to Archelaüs[5] and spent time there and pleased the king by writing a play bearing his name. He gained success there and was placed in charge of financial administration.

He is said to have grown a long beard and to have had moles around his eyes; and to have married firstly Melito and secondly Choerile and to have left three sons, the eldest Mnesarchides, a merchant, next Mnesilochus an actor, and the youngest Euripides who produced some of his father's plays.

---

[1] Again, different readings of the text (reading φρύγει τι and τὰ φρύγαν' for Φρυγικὸν, may suggest the rather more colourful reading: 'Mnesilochus roasts some fresh drama for Euripides as Socrates lays the firewood'.

[2] Hellanicus of Mytilene, a lexicographer.

[3] Magnesia: in the region of Thessalia in Northern Greece.

[4] The privileges related to 'proxenia', a legal status of friendship offered to a foreigner.

[5] Archelaüs, King of Macedonia.

He began to produce plays in the archonship of Callias in the first year after the 81st Olympiad[1]. His first play was *Peliades*[2] when he also won third prize. In all he wrote 92 plays of which 78 are extant. Of these, three are spurious: Tennes, Rhadamanthys and Peirithous.

He died, according to Philochorus, when over 70 years old, and according to Eratosthenes, aged 75. He was buried in Macedonia. A cenotaph was raised to him in Athens and there was an inscription on it written either by the historian Thucydides or the songwriter Timotheus: "All Greece is a memorial of Euripides. His bones/ are in the land of Macedonia; for there he came to the end of his life./ His homeland was Athens, the Greece of Greece. Most of all, the Muses/ he pleased and receives praise from many." They say both memorials were struck by lightning.

They say that Sophocles, hearing that he had died, went out in a grey or purple cloak and that he had his chorus and actors enter the ceremonial parade without garlands and that the people wept.

III. They say that he kitted out a cave on Salamis with its entrance facing out to sea, and there he spent his days, fleeing the crowds. Hence, he took most of his analogies from the sea.

He appeared to be sullen, grave and crabby as well as laughter-hating and misogynistic. This led Aristophanes to condemn him: "Euripides seems to me to be sour to talk to".

They say he married Choerile, the daughter of Mnesilochus and having in mind how disreputable she was, he firstly wrote the play *Hippolytus* in which he displayed, as in triumph, the shamelessness of women, and then he divorced her. Her second husband said "She acts properly for me", to which Euripides replied, "You are an unfortunate man if you think that the same wife acts properly for one husband but not for another".

[1] 455 BC.

[2] *Peliades* or *Daughters of Pelias*.

They say that he married a second wife whom he found to be more disreputable than the first and so became even bolder in his defamation of women. Women wanted to kill him, going into the cave where he continued to write.

Jealous allegations were made that Cephisophon co-wrote his tragedies.

Hermippus says that after the death of Euripides, Dionysus the tyrant of Sicily sent a talent to his heirs for him to take his harp, writing tablet and stylus, and that when he saw them, he ordered those who brought them to hang them in the shrine of the Muses, inscribing them with his and Euripides' names. For this reason Euripides was called 'most loved by foreigners' since he was loved most especially by foreigners. The Athenians were jealous of him. When a rather uneducated youth out of envy said he had bad breath, "Now, now," he said "my mouth is sweeter than honey and the Sirens."

Ib. Euripides, the son of Mnesarchides, an Athenian: the comic poets mocked him as the son of a vegetable seller. They say that to begin with he was a painter, but having studied under Archelaüs, the natural scientist, and Anaxagoras, he moved towards writing tragedies. Being of a rather haughty disposition, he naturally shunned the populace and was unconcerned about popularity in the theatre. As a result, this caused him harm, but helped Sophocles in equal measure. The comic poets attacked him and, out of envy, tore him to pieces. Disdaining all this, he left for Macedonia – to King Archelaüs, where, returning rather late one evening he was killed by the king's dogs. He began to produce plays in the year of the 81st Olympiad[1] in the archonship of Callias.

---

[1] Ie. the first year after eighty-first Olympiad, 455 BC, as reported above in Ia.

He wrote 92 plays in all of which 67 are extant; there are a further three of disputed authorship. Eight are satyr plays of which one is of disputed authorship[1]. He won five victories. Employing a moderately formal style, he excelled in expressiveness, setting out sharply both sides of an argument. He was unequalled in his lyrical writing, surpassing almost all lyric poets. But in his dialogues he was awkward and burdensome and in his prologues irksome. He was particularly rhetorical in the setting out of arguments, with embroidered language, and ready to refute what had already been said.

II. He died in the following way: In Macedonia is a village called Thracon on account of Thracians once settling there. A Molossian hound of Archelaüs entered the village and wandered about. The Thracians, as was their custom, slaughtered and ate it. Archelaüs fined them a talent. Since they did not have that sum, they asked Euripides to seek a release from their debt to the king. A little later, when Euripides was walking in a certain grove outside the city, and Archelaüs came past hunting, the huntsmen set their dogs free and these attacked Euripides, and the poet was torn apart and eaten. The dogs were the offspring of the dog taken by the Thracians, whence the Macedonian saying of "dog's justice".

IV. He mocked women in his plays on account of the following: He had a homebred slave called Cephisophon, with whom he accused his own wife of behaving disreputably. To begin with he succeeded in discouraging her. But since he could not persuade her, he left his wife to him, and Cephisophon wanted to have her. Aristophanes said: "Best and blackest Cephisophon/ you sit alongside Euripides in most things/ and you co-write his songs."

---

[1] This section appears to say that there were 95 plays in total of which three were of disputed authorship. 67 of the undisputed plays were extant. Of the 95 plays, eight were satyr plays (of which one was of disputed authorship). This does not accord with Ia above which states there were 92 plays in all of which three were of disputed authorship; it further states that 78 were extant.

They say that women, on account of his criticisms which he made of them in his writings, attacked him at the Thesmophoria[1] and wanted to do away with him. But they spared him firstly because of the Muses and secondly because he promised not to speak ill of them ever again. And in *Melanippe*, he says this of them: "A criticism made by men of women/ twangs an empty bow and is a poor speech./ They are better than men, so I say."

Philemon so loved him that he dared to say about his death: "If the dead in truth/ have perception as some men say/ I would hang myself so as to see Euripides."

---

[1] Thesmophoria: a festival associated with the sowing or harvesting of the crops. It honoured Demeter and Persephone. The participants were limited to adult women.

Structure of *Iphigenia at Aulis*

	Lines		Page
Prologue	*1* -	*163*	23
Entrance of the Chorus		*164*	28
First choral song	*164* -	*302*	28
First episode	*303* -	*542*	31
Second choral song	*543* -	*606*	40
Second episode	*607* -	*750*	42
Third choral song	*751* -	*800*	49
Third episode	*801* -	*1035*	51
Fourth choral song	*1036* -	*1097*	59
Lament	*(1080* -	*1097*	60
Conclusion	*1098* -	*1629*	61
Sung lament	*(1276* -	*1335)*	67
Sung lament	*(1475* -	*1531)*	76

Iphigenia at Aulis

Dramatis personae[1]

Agamemnon

Old man

Chorus

Menelaüs

Messenger

Clytemnestra

Iphigenia

Achilles

Second Messenger

---

[1] The Dramatis Personae are set out as in the transmitted editions. More fully explained, they are:
Agamemnon, King of Mycenae; Old man, in the service of Agamemnon; Chorus of women of Chalcis; Menelaüs, King of Sparta; Messenger, in the service of Clytemnestra; Clytemnestra, wife of Agamemnon; Iphigenia, daughter of Agamemnon and Clytemnestra; Achilles, King of Phthia and the Myrmidons; Second messenger, a Greek soldier.
Non-speaking parts: Attendants, accompanying Clytemnestra; a band of warriors accompanying Achilles; a band of Agamemnon's men.

The three principle actors take parts as follows: Protagonist: Agamemnon, Achilles; Deuteragonist: Menelaüs, Clytemnestra; Tritagonist: Iphigenia, Old man, Messengers.

Iphigenia at Aulis

Scene: The Greek camp at Aulis; The entrance to the tent of King Agamemnon opens on to the stage. A path leads to the camp itself. A path in the other direction leads away from the camp.

Time: Before dawn. The Greek army has assembled to set sail for Troy.

PROLOGUE

(*Enter* Agamemnon *from his tent, distressed and holding a letter which has been sealed and reopened*)

AGAMEMNON Old man, come here to my tent!

(*Enter* Old Man *along the path*)

OLD MAN I'm coming. What new ideas have you now, King
    Agamemnon?
AGAMEMNON Hurry!
OLD MAN I am hurrying. An old man like me cannot sleep in
    any case.
AGAMEMNON Look at the stars that cross the sky. Look there,
    at Sirius rising up by the seven stars of the Pleiades, and
    still in mid-heaven.
    Listen!
    There is no sound – neither of birds nor of the sea. The
    silence of the winds keeps us captive here by the Euripus
    Strait.
OLD MAN Why are *you* getting up and leaving your tent, King
    Agamemnon? All remains peaceful here at Aulis. The
    guards are at their posts. Let us go inside.

AGAMEMNON I envy you, old man. I envy the man who lives his life through without risk, himself unknown and without renown. Those in authority I envy less.

OLD MAN Yes, but authority is a noble thing.

AGAMEMNON Authority is noble but vulnerable. Honour is sweet, but accompanied by grief. If a king disturbs the gods, they overturn his life; and his fickle subjects are soon displeased and grind him down.

OLD MAN Kings cannot think like that, Agamemnon, and your father Atreus could hardly ensure that everything in your life was to be to your taste. There will be times of happiness and times of pain. You are only a man, and, though you may not want it, the will of the gods will prevail.

But, I saw the light in your tent, and I see you have written a letter which you hold in your hand – but here the writing is blurred. You have sealed the letter but broken it open again; (*seeing dirt on the letter*) you have thrown it to the ground, and (*looking at Agamemnon*) you have wept so many tears that your distraction has brought you close to madness.

What is the matter? What has happened, my king? Come, share the problem with me. You are speaking to a good and trusted man. Remember your father-in-law, Tyndareüs, sent me to serve you, when you married his daughter. He knew my loyalty.

AGAMEMNON Listen then!

There were three sisters, Phoebe, Clytemnestra, who became my wife, and Helen.

Helen attracted suitors from amongst the leading families of Greece. The suitors' rivalry was so intense that they began threatening to kill each other. Helen's father, Tyndareüs, did not know what to do for the best. But then he had the idea of having all the suitors swear vows, solemnized by burnt sacrificial offerings, that, whichever of them married Helen, they would all join together to defend him in the event that anyone ever came to seize her from her home and from her husband; and that they would wage war on, and destroy, any such person's city, Greek or barbarian, with their armies.

They all made these vows – a clever piece of thinking on Tyndareüs' part – and then he allowed Helen to follow Aphrodite's beckoning and choose one of her suitors as a husband. She chose and married my brother, Menelaüs, king of Sparta.

I wish she had not!

But then there came to Sparta, from the city of Troy, a man whom men say had judged goddesses, Prince Paris, dressed to suit his handsome youthfulness, in shimmering gold and barbarian finery. Finding Menelaüs away from home, he seduced Helen, who was all too willing to be seduced, and took her away to his lands around Trojan Mount Ida.

Menelaüs, her husband, sped throughout Greece in a rage, citing the ancient vows exacted by Helen's father, and demanding help in the face of injustice.

Thereupon, the Greeks rose up with their spears and armaments, and they assembled here at the straits, at the bnay of Aulis, arrayed with ships and shields, horses and chariots. They made me their general, being Menelaüs' brother. How I wish someone else had taken command instead of me!

The army was mustered and ready, but we waited at Aulis, our ships becalmed.

As we continued in this plight, unable to set sail, Calchas the priest and seer announced that the Goddess Artemis, the deity inhabiting that place, had demanded the ritual sacrifice of my own daughter, Iphigenia. He said that only after this sacrifice, would the Goddess allow us to sail on our way to sack Troy: but that without the sacrifice of my daughter, there would be no success.

When I had heard what Calchas had to say, I ordered my herald, Talthybius, to proclaim in the clearest terms the disbanding of the armies, since I could never bring myself to kill my own daughter.

But, at this point, my brother, using every argument he could muster, persuaded me to do the unthinkable. I sent a message to my wife to send my daughter here – on the pretext of marrying Achilles. I wrote admiringly of the reputation of this great warrior and claimed that he was refusing to sail with the Greeks unless we sent a bride from our family to him at his native Phthia. Yes, that was the means of persuasion I had to have my wife send our daughter here. Of the Greeks, only Calchas, Odysseus, Menelaüs and I myself know the truth.

I knew my instructions were ill-judged then, but anyway, now I am countermanding them by this letter, which I have written tonight and which you have seen me open and now reseal, old man. (*reseals the letter*)

Now take this letter to my wife in Mycenae.

(*gives Old Man the letter*)

AGAMEMNON I will tell you all that is written in it, since you are loyal to my wife and my family.

OLD MAN Yes, tell me the contents of the letter so that I may speak to them accordingly.

AGAMEMNON The message reads:

"Clytemnestra, I send this letter to countermand my earlier one. Do not send your daughter to the calm bay of Aulis by the straits off Euboea. Another time will come for us to celebrate our child's wedding."

OLD MAN If Achilles has been deprived of his marriage, surely he will vent his anger on you and your wife. That would be dangerous. What do you say?

AGAMEMNON No, no. I simply used Achilles' name. Achilles knows nothing of the supposed marriage or my scheme, or that I indicated that I would give my daughter to him in marriage.

OLD MAN You were taking a terrible risk, King Agamemnon – leading her here to be sacrificed for the Greeks, with a promise of marriage to the son of a goddess.

AGAMEMNON Ah! I am losing my mind; the gods are driving me mad!

But hurry on your way. Make no concession to old age.

OLD MAN I will hurry, my king.

AGAMEMNON Do not sit and rest by woodland springs nor let sleep cast its spell on you.

OLD MAN Be calm.

AGAMEMNON Be on the lookout when paths diverge and make sure that no carriage carrying my daughter passes by you unseen, as it rolls along towards our ships.

OLD MAN I will.

AGAMEMNON Start your journey. And if you meet with her and her companions, seize the reins of their carriage and send them back to their homes in Mycenae.

OLD MAN Will I be trusted by your wife and child?

AGAMEMNON Keep the seal on the letter you carry safe.

Go now. See, the sky is brightening with the light of dawn and the coming blaze of the sun.

You must help me now in my troubles.

(*Exit* Old Man *along the path away from the camp*)

AGAMEMNON How I realise that no mortal man is, in the end, happy or blessed. No-one yet has been born to a life without grief.

(*Exit* Agamemnon *into his tent.*)

ENTRANCE OF THE CHORUS

(*Enter the* Chorus, *excited at seeing the Greek armies.*)

FIRST CHORAL SONG

[164]
CHORUS   *[strophe A]*
  We've made our way to the headland here,
  the sands of Aulis' sea-girt bay.
  Through waves in the straits of Euripus
  our ship's deep keels straight furrows ploughed
  as we our home in Chalcis left,
  the source of waters flowing clear
  from famous Arethusa's springs.
  The fearsome armies of the Greeks,
  the fleet that's rowed by demigods,
  against the citadel of Troy
  in a thousand ships of crafted pine
  (as our husbands say, as news has spread)
  the red-haired Menelaüs sends
  with Agamemnon at its head.
  The beauteous Helen is their goal
  whom rustic Paris stole away
  from Sparta's reedy river banks,
  his gift from Aphrodite's hand.
  For he, by watery springs, as judge
  of beauty of goddesses three,
  to Aphrodite gave the prize.

            [antistrophe A]

  We fled the grove of Artemis,
  by human sacrifice made red.
  As women young, we blushed to see
  (though willingly, we must admit)
  the rows of shields, the swords and spears
  the tents arrayed along the shore,
  the horse, the armour of the Greeks!

We saw there Ajax, Oeleus' son,
and Ajax, son of Telemon
their warlike plans in council lay;
Protesilaös games of draughts,
with chequered board and pieces bright,
'gainst godly Palamedes played,
descendant of Poseidon's line;
and Diomede the discus hurled,
beside him there was Meriones,
descendant of the God of War,
his figure broad so fine to see;
Odysseus next, Laërtes' son
from island home, with Nireus stood,
most handsome of the warrior Greeks.

[epode]

Achilles, th'equal of the wind,
the fleetest runner of them all,
whom Thetis bore and Chiron trained,
we saw along the shingle sprint.
In armour full, at speed, he raced
against a team of horses fast
intent on claiming victory!
But Eumelos the charioteer
with shouts, his four-horse team urged on.
The horses (fine as any seen),
with harnesses of glittering gold,
the inner pair with dappled coats,
all flecked with white and the outer two,
both bays with fetlocks flickering bright
to the whip at the turn, to the post did fly,
to the traces did gallop and gallop and strain;
Yet still, Achilles, fully armed,
beside the horses, striving forth
kept even pace, each muscle taut,
uncompromising to prevail,
and level with the chariot rail
and axles, on he ran.

[strophe B]

We viewed the ships – a wondrous sight:
we most impressive found them all:
the Myrmidons were on the right:
they seemed as Gods of War.

[antistrophe B]

And next to these were sixty moored
from Athens, fame for Theseus' son,
each with Athene's image high
above the stern so fierce.

[strophe C]

Then next, appeared Boeotian ships;
a fleet of fifty there we saw.
And Cadmus lit their lofty sterns
with golden serpent's gleam.

[antistrophe C]

One hundred Mycenean ships
were ranged, by Agamemnon led,
to gain redress for a wife that's fled
with vile barbarian prince.

[epode]

Then ships from Nestor's Pylos lay:
from Phocis, Locris, Aenia,
from Taphos, Elis, Salamis,
are come the countless ships.
  We pity the barbarian who
  his fleet against the Greek commands.
  No homecoming for him awaits,
  but only unkind Fate.

FIRST EPISODE

(*Enter* Old Man *hurrying back from the way he went with Agamemnon's letter, and* Menelaüs, *holding a rod of office, pursuing him. Menelaüs seizes hold of Agamemnon's letter.*)

[303]

OLD MAN Menelaüs! You are venturing into matters you should not! (*attempts constantly to recover the letter*)

MENELAUS Leave hold.
    (*pushes Old Man away; breaks the seal and reads the letter*)
    You are far too loyal to your masters.

OLD MAN You reproach me with something to my credit.

MENELAUS You will regret it, if you do not do as you should.

OLD MAN It was not for you to open the letter which I was carrying.

MENELAUS Nor for you to bring ruin on the whole Greek enterprise.

OLD MAN Discuss that with others. Get your hands off that letter.

MENELAUS I will not.

OLD MAN Nor shall I let go.

MENELAUS I shall soon be cracking you head open with this rod.

OLD MAN Dying for one's master is a noble death.

MENELAUS Leave off. You have far too much to say for a slave.

(*Enter* Agamemnon *from his tent.*)

OLD MAN My king, we are being wronged. He snatched your letter from my hand. Agamemnon, his actions are outrageous.

AGAMEMNON What is all this noise and disturbance?

MENELAUS My account of this affair, not his, is the one that will be heard.

31

AGAMEMNON Menelaüs, what is your argument with this man? Why did you attack him?

MENELAUS Look me in the eye; then I will tell you the reason.

AGAMEMNON Are you suggesting that I, the son of Atreus, cannot look you in the eye?

MENELAUS You see this letter? It contains a message that will bring disgrace.

(*Agamemnon beckons to Old Man to leave.*
Exit Old Man *into Agamemnon's tent.*)

AGAMEMNON I can see it and I require its return.

MENELAUS Not until I have explained its contents to the Greek armies.

AGAMEMNON What's that?! Have you broken the seal, and read what you should not?

MENELAUS Yes, I have opened it, and I know you will be embarrassed by having your secret plans made known to all.

AGAMEMNON But where did you find it? Ye Gods! What shamelessness!

MENELAUS I was waiting for your daughter and her escort coming from Mycenae.

AGAMEMNON What business is that of yours? Look to your own affairs.

MENELAUS My wanting to make it my business has clearly provoked you. Remember I am not your slave.

AGAMEMNON We are in a sorry state, are we not? Am I not to manage my own affairs?

MENELAUS You are a crook; you were, you are now and you always will be.

AGAMEMNON You are clever in your slander. How you must begrudge the truth.

MENELAUS A mind that is not resolute is unjust, and friends find its intentions unclear. I need to be certain about you. Anger must not divert you from the truth, nor am I questioning your resolve unreasonably.

32

You know how eager you were to lead the Greeks against Troy: you pretended you were not, but in reality you were. How humble you were – shaking everyone by the hand, opening your doors to all your subjects, conversing with everyone, whether they wanted to or not. That was how you sought to purchase the approbation of all.

But then, when you had obtained the command, your attitude changed. You were not so friendly as before. You were no longer approachable; rarely at home to welcome visitors.

But a worthy man, who attains high rank, should not change in this way, but should consider it important that he remain a reliable friend, particularly since his success best enables him to be of help to his friends.

This was the first cause for complaint you gave: but then, when you arrived at Aulis with the allied armies of all Greece, you were weak, allowing the lack of a fair breeze – ill-luck from the gods – to undermine your resolve. The Greeks asked for the fleet to be dispersed and sent home rather than labour on at Aulis. How unhappy and dejected your expression was! To think that you commanded a thousand ships but that your armies would never fill the Trojan plain! You used to ask me "What shall I do?" and "How am I going to find a way out of this?" Your fear was loss of command and of your noble reputation.

Then, when Calchas said you should give your daughter to the Goddess Artemis by ritual sacrifice, and thus enable the Greeks to sail on to Troy, you were delighted, and happily promised to sacrifice the girl. You willingly sent word to your wife to arrange for the girl to be brought here on the pretext of marriage to Achilles. You were under no coercion – do not say you were.

And now, having made that promise, you have been caught writing another letter with quite a different message. Do you not now say that you will no longer be your daughter's killer? Indeed you do. The air around us can bear witness.

You are not alone in being a king and failing. Many others have attempted to conduct affairs of state, only to abandon the work ignobly – sometimes because of the witless opposition of their fellow citizens, but often because of their own inabilities.

I weep for wretched Greece: her noble intent is thwarted by you and your daughter in the face of a few mocking barbarian nobodies!

No-one should be given the command an army by playing politics. Generalship requires far greater mental qualities.

CHORUS

How terrible for brothers thus to fall
to arguments and fights, when brought to strife.

AGAMEMNON   And I have a few unpleasant things to say to you. I shall, however, talk sensibly, as your brother, without indulging in your haughty poses. A man of worth must have a sense of propriety.

Tell me, why this threatening appearance with your face blood-red with anger? Who has wronged you? What is it you want? Do you want a virtuous wife? It is not for me to provide you with one: and you made a poor job of looking after what you had. Am I to pay the penalty for your inadequacies? – I'm not the one has acted wrongly.

It is not my success which troubles you. No, you merely want the embrace of a beautiful wife, irrespective of the consequences – or decency. Worthless pleasures for a worthless man.

On the other hand, am I mad, having made a bad decision, to have changed my mind? No. If anyone is mad, it is you, who, having lost a bad wife, want to get her back! Why? The gods did you a favour.

The misguided, marriage-seeking suitors swore their oath – Tyndareüs saw to that – and, in my opinion, you can thank the god of Hope, certainly not your own abilities. You have your allies – wage your war. They are ready –

and weak in the head. But the gods are not fools – they can recognise vows entered into foolishly and under compulsion.

And I will not kill my own children. Nor is it sensible for you to act ignobly to avenge your wife.

The days and nights would see me waste away in tears, if I acted towards my own flesh and blood in defiance of all law and morality.

That is all I have to say to you. My views are clear and simple. You may not wish to act sensibly, but I do.

CHORUS
> I see that his intentions now have changed;
> but that is for the good: it spares his child.

MENELAUS Ah! I do not have the friends I thought I had.

AGAMEMNON Not if you are happy to see them killed.

MENELAUS Would you still claim to have the same father as I?

AGAMEMNON I would be pleased to share inherited wisdom not weakness.

MENELAUS Should not friends share friends' sorrow?

AGAMEMNON Ask my help in any noble enterprise, but not in engineering my own ruin.

MENELAUS Do you not think that you should labour for the benefit of Greece?

AGAMEMNON The gods have condemned Greece to the same disease as you.

MENELAUS Boast of your command and betray your brother. I shall adopt other plans – and other friends…

(*Enter* Messenger, *along the path leading away from the camp, interrupting Menelaus' speech*)

[*second half of line* 414]

MESSENGER (*brightly*) Agamemnon, leader of the Panhellenic armies, I have come, bringing with me, as you requested, your daughter Iphigenia.

(*not noticing the shocked looks of Agamemnon*) Her
mother, the lady Clytemnestra accompanies her – and
your baby son Orestes. I am sure you would wish to see
them all after being away from home for so long.

After their long journey, they are refreshing themselves by
the waters of a spring. The ponies are resting also – we put
them in a grassy meadow for them to graze.

I have come in advance to you to enable you to prepare to
receive them.

Word of your daughter's arrival travelled quickly through
the army and the men soon crowded round to see her. Yes,
those favoured by the gods become famous and attract the
attention of everyone. Questions are on everyone's lips:
"Is it a wedding? Is something happening? Or has King
Agamemnon summoned his daughter here simply because
he wants to see her?" Many have guessed at a wedding
and point out that offerings are traditionally made to
Artemis, the goddess of Aulis, before a marriage, and so,
"Who is she going to marry?" they ask.

So come, make a start to the rites with sacred bread,
garland your heads, and you, King Menelaüs, prepare the
wedding hymn, and let the sound of the flute resound
throughout the camp, and let us hear the sound of dancing
feet. For this is to be a happy day for the maid!

AGAMEMNON You have my thanks: but go inside my tent. All
will be well as Fate takes its course.

(*Exit* Messenger *into Agamemnon's tent*)

AGAMEMNON What can I say in my misfortune? Where can I
begin? I have fallen under the yoke of necessity. Divine
fortune has outwitted me in my plans.

How low birth has its advantages! Shedding tears and
telling of sorrows come easy to the low-born. We men of
noble birth have our unhappiness, but the weight of our
dignity stands monitor of our lives - and the people have

36

us as their slaves. I am ashamed to shed a tear, but am ashamed not to weep at the enormity of what faces me.

What shall I say to my wife? How shall I receive her? How am I to look her in the face? By coming to this disaster unannounced, she has completed my destruction.

Of course she accompanied her daughter to her wedding – to perform the dearest duties of a mother. But here she finds us in the direst predicament.

How I pity the poor maid – why do I call her a maid? For Death, it seems, will soon have her as a bride. She will soon be begging me: "Father, are you to kill me? Is this the marriage you have arranged for me with the help of your friends?"

My baby son, Orestes, who is nearby, will cry out unintelligible words so full of understanding.

That marriage with Helen has destroyed me: Priam's son Paris is the cause of that.

CHORUS
> And I have pity too, a stranger here,
> and grieve to see misfortunes of a king.

MENELAUS Brother, give me your right hand.
AGAMEMNON So be it; (*they clasp right hands*) you have won and I am defeated.
MENELAUS I swear by my and your grandfather, Pelops, the father of Atreus, that I speak to you from the heart, sensibly and with no ulterior motive, and that I say what I know is right.

> I saw the tear fall from your eye. I felt pity and let a tear fall in turn from mine.

> I withdraw what I said just now. I am no threat to you.

> I see matters from your point of view; and I urge you not to kill your child nor let my interests predominate. It would be unjust for you to weep whilst all is well for me; for yours to die whilst mine enjoy life's light.

What do I want? If I desire marriage, could I not have my choice of bride elsewhere?

Am I to lose a brother – nothing could be worse – as I recover Helen – am I to exchange good for bad?

I spoke rashly as a young man does. But now, with clearer sight, I see what it is to kill one's own child. Besides, I feel pity for the poor girl – she is my own kin – who is about to be sacrificed for the sake of my marriage. But of what relevance is Helen to your daughter?

Disband the armies and let the men leave Aulis. Brother, dry your tears and let me cease weeping also.

If your daughter is in any way the object of a god's commands, let it not be on my account! I defer my interest to yours.

But is this a change of heart from my former excess? You are my brother and I love my kin. And it is not the mark of an evil man to pursue always what is best.

CHORUS
How nobly spoken as a man of rank,
disgracing not great Tantalus or Zeus!

AGAMEMNON You have my thanks, Menelaüs. I did not expect to receive such consideration from you. It does you credit.

Love or family rivalries may cause brothers to quarrel. And I abhor such bitterness amongst close kin.

However, we must face the necessity of fortune – the bloody slaughter of my daughter!

MENELAUS What?! What makes her death a necessity?

AGAMEMNON The assembly of all the Greek armies.

MENELAUS Not if you send her back to Mycenae.

AGAMEMNON I could send her home without their knowing; but I cannot avoid a further matter.

MENELAUS What is that? You must not be too fearful of the masses.

AGAMEMNON Calchas will tell the armies of the Goddess' commands.

MENELAUS Not if he's dead first!
    It can easily be arranged.
AGAMEMNON There is another matter… Do you not see?
MENELAUS You must tell me, if I am to understand.
AGAMEMNON Odysseus knows everything.
MENELAUS Odysseus will not hurt either you or me.
AGAMEMNON But he is always subtle – and takes the side of the mob.
MENELAUS Yes, and he is dangerously ambitious.
AGAMEMNON Can you not see him standing before all the assembled armies, telling them in detail of Calchas and the demands of the Goddess; and that I had promised a sacrifice to Artemis; and then that I had have gone back on my word? Will he not carry the armies with him and order them to kill you and me and then slaughter my daughter? Even if I escape to Mycenae protected by its Cyclopean walls, they will come and ravage my lands and wreak utter destruction.

Such is the desperate plight I face at the hands of the gods. But one thing you must make sure of, Menelaüs. When you go about the armies, on no account must my wife Clytemnestra learn anything of what is happening, until I have taken my child and sent her on her way to Death and Hades. The fewest tears must accompany my evil deed.

(*to Chorus*) And you, ladies, must be quiet as well.

(*Exeunt* Agamemnon *into his tent and* Menelaüs *along the path to the camp.*)

SECOND CHORAL SONG

[543]
CHORUS   *[strophe]*

    How blest are they who can enjoy
    the virtuous mean, by wisdom gained,
    of Aphrodite's gift of Love,
    and who with quiet calm avoid
    the frenzied gadfly passions, wrought
    by gold-haired Eros' arrows twain
    that fly so fleetly us to charm:
    one gives a life of happiness,
    but one a life confused and rent.
    O beauteous Cyprian Goddess keep
    that last away from my soft bed
    as moderation is my guide.
    May I in grace and holy joys
    in Aphrodite's bounty share
    but all unwise excess avoid.

                                       [antistrophe]

    Such varied natures mortals have,
    such varied ways; but nobleness
    for ever to us stands out clear.
    Its thoughtful nurture always strives
    with import great towards the good.
    And modesty marks out the wise,
    encompassing that grace so rare,
    which causes us by judgment sound
    to see our duty, which in turn
    renown undying guarantees.
    Virtue must be pursued by all:
    no secret loves must women have,
    and men must all have this great aim,
    that, striving in a thousand ways,
    they yet enhance their city's fame.

You came, O Paris Prince of Troy,
a cowherd 'midst white heifers raised
on Ida's grassy mountain slopes,
a-playing on barbarian pipes
just as that famed Olympus played,
his music made, on Phrygian reeds.
Whilst tending to your well-grazed herds,
your judgment you were called to give
on three goddess's rivalry,
which led you on to the ivory throne
of Helen, who with fluttering eyes
on you did gaze, your love returned.
So now you bring the Greeks to war,
to gather here with spears and ships,
to fight and strive against your land,
against the citadel of Troy.

See, see the blessèd of the blest!
The daughter of the Queen we see,
Iphigenia, princess, comes
with Clytemnestra, royal born!
From noble kings they trace their line
and greater fame their destiny!
The powerful appear as gods
to such as us, less fortunate.

So let we, Chalcis' women, stand,
await the carriage of the Queen.
We'll lend our hands with kind intent,
and help them from their carriage step.
O gentle Agamemnon's child,
be not afraid as you draw near,
though strangers, we, as hosts to guests,
shall nothing do to cause alarm.

SECOND EPISODE

(*Enter* Clytemnestra *and* Iphigenia *with* Attendants. *They are revealed to be sitting in a carriage having travelled along the road that leads away from the camp. Clytemnestra holds a baby. A bird is heard to sing on her right-hand side.*)

[607]

CLYTEMNESTRA (*hearing the bird song*) That birdsong: what a wonderful, auspicious welcome for us! And what hopes I have! I bring my daughter as bride to a noble marriage!

(*to her Attendants*) Come down from our carriage. I have brought a dowry with me for my daughter: help to take it into our lodgings.

(*The* Attendants *descend from the carriage with bags of gold*)

(*to Iphigenia*) But first, my child, step down carefully from the carriage. Mind your pretty legs! Take care not to hurt yourself!

(*to her Attendants*) You young women, help her down from the carriage. One of you, give me the support of your hand so that I can climb down also.

(*the Attendants help Clytemnestra and Iphigenia*)

Some of you, stand at the ponies' head: they are easily frightened when none is by to calm them.

(*Some of the* Attendants *comply*)

(*to an Attendant*) And will you take hold of Agamemnon's son, baby Orestes. (*looking at the baby she carries*) You are asleep, my child – the carriage has rocked you to sleep. But you must wake for the happy wedding of your sister: you are gaining a noble brother-in-law, Achilles, grandson of godlike Nereus.

(*Then Clytemnestra hands Orestes to an Attendant; Clytemnestra and Iphigenia alight from the carriage.*)

(*to Iphigenia*) Sit here by my feet, my child, and as you sit close by me, show these young women (*indicating the Chorus*) how happy we are!

(*Iphigenia sits at Clytemnestra's feet.*
Exit an Attendant *with the carriage to their lodgings away from the camp. The other Attendants remain, one holding Orestes.*
Then: Enter Agamemnon *from his tent*)

CLYTEMNESTRA But greet your dear father.
Agamemnon, my dear husband and lord, we have arrived – as you directed.
IPHIGENIA Oh mother, I love being close to you, but do not be angry if I embrace my father.
(*rushes to embrace Agamemnon*)
Father, I do so want to embrace you after all this time!
(*but Agamemnon does not return the embrace*)
But do not be annoyed.
CLYTEMNESTRA Do embrace him, child. Of all my children, you were always closest to your father.
IPHIGENIA Father, how pleased I am to see you after such a long time!
AGAMEMNON And I, your father, am pleased to see you. You speak for both of us.
IPHIGENIA You did *well*, father, to bring me out here.
AGAMEMNON I am too overcome to speak to you, my child.
IPHIGENIA Oh! You look so careworn – and we are so happy to be re-united.
AGAMEMNON A king and a war-leader has much on his mind.
IPHIGENIA Think of me and forget your cares for now.
AGAMEMNON I do think of you and nothing else.
IPHIGENIA Calm your angry expression and look kindly on me.
AGAMEMNON My child, seeing you, I have rejoiced – as much as I have rejoiced.
IPHIGENIA Why then are tears falling from your eyes?
AGAMEMNON Because of the long separation – which awaits us.
IPHIGENIA Why? Where do these Trojans live?

43

AGAMEMNON   Trojan Paris should not be alive to live anywhere!

IPHIGENIA You will cause us to be far apart, then, when you leave me, father?

AGAMEMNON   Your all too knowing words bring me great grief.

IPHIGENIA I will speak nonsense if it brings you happiness!

AGAMEMNON (*aside*) Ah, hiding the truth is unbearable!
   (*to Clytemnestra*) I thank you for coming.

IPHIGENIA But father, remain at home with your children!

AGAMEMNON I wish I could; and it grieves me that I cannot.

IPHIGENIA May Menelaüs and his evil troubles and his weapons all perish!

AGAMEMNON (*aside*) What has destroyed me will soon destroy others.

IPHIGENIA You have been away such a long time here in the bay of Aulis.

AGAMEMNON And even now I am prevented from sending my armies forward.

IPHIGENIA I wish you and I could sail off together!

AGAMEMNON A different journey awaits you – one in which you will remember your father.

IPHIGENIA Am I to journey with my mother or alone?

AGAMEMNON Alone. You will be apart from your father and your mother.

IPHIGENIA You are not going to send me to live somewhere else, are you father?

AGAMEMNON   That's enough! Such matters are not for young girls.

IPHIGENIA Hurry back from Troy, father, when all is finished there.

AGAMEMNON But first I have to make a sacrifice here.

IPHIGENIA Of course, one must observe religious duty.

AGAMEMNON You will see. You will be standing by the sacred water.

IPHIGENIA Will we perform sacred dances around the altar, father?

AGAMEMNON (*turns away, aside*) I envy you your ignorance.
(*to Iphigenia*) Go to your lodgings – young girls should not be seen outdoors: but first give me your hand and a kiss. You will soon be apart from your father for all too long.
What heart, what cheeks, what fine fair hair! How hateful the city of Troy becomes to me – and Helen!
I must stop talking; I can feel the tears in my eyes.
Go to your lodgings.

(*Exit* Iphigenia *and* Attendants *along the path to their lodgings. One or more Attendants remain, with Orestes.*)

AGAMEMNON (*to Clytemnestra*) I beg your pardon for all this, Clytemnestra, if I seem over-wrought at the prospect of – giving my daughter in marriage to Achilles. A daughter's leaving may be blessed by the gods, but it still bites at a parent's heart – when you have laboured long and hard for her – to see her go to another's home.
CLYTEMNESTRA I am not so foolish as to think I will not suffer in exactly the same way when I escort my daughter to the sound of the wedding hymn. Of course I do not reproach you: time, as life goes on, will assuage your sadness.
Now, I know the name of the youth to whom you have betrothed our daughter, but tell me of his parents and his country. I'm dying to know!
AGAMEMNON His great-grandmother was Aegina, daughter of the river god, Asopus.
CLYTEMNESTRA Oh, and who did she marry?
AGAMEMNON She married Zeus and bore a son Aeacus.
CLYTEMNESTRA And which child of Aeacus was his heir?
AGAMEMNON That was Peleus. He married Thetis, the daughter of Nereus.
CLYTEMNESTRA Did a god give her or did he take her by force?

45

AGAMEMNON Zeus himself gave Thetis in marriage and her father consented.

CLYTEMNESTRA And where was the wedding? Was it by the sea?

AGAMEMNON They were married in Chiron's home at the foot of Mount Pelium.

CLYTEMNESTRA Is not that where they say the Centaurs live?

AGAMEMNON Yes, and that is where the gods celebrated the marriage of Peleus.

CLYTEMNESTRA Was Achilles brought up by his mother, Thetis, or his father?

AGAMEMNON By Chiron – so that he would not learn evil ways.

CLYTEMNESTRA A wise teacher; and a wise parent to find such a teacher.

AGAMEMNON Well, such a man will be your daughter's husband.

CLYTEMNESTRA A sound choice: and where in Greece does he live?

AGAMEMNON By the river Apidanus in Phthia.

CLYTEMNESTRA Will they live there after the marriage?

AGAMEMNON That will be his choice.

CLYTEMNESTRA And may they be very happy! Now, when is the marriage to take place?

AGAMEMNON At the time of the next full moon.

CLYTEMNESTRA And have you made the initial wedding sacrifices to the goddess?

AGAMEMNON I am about to do it. As it happens, I was just getting prepared.

CLYTEMNESTRA And afterwards, are we to have a marriage feast?

AGAMEMNON When I have sacrificed what I have to sacrifice to the gods.

CLYTEMNESTRA Will there be a feast for the women?

AGAMEMNON Yes; down by the ships.

CLYTEMNESTRA (*disappointed*) I suppose that's the proper setting.

AGAMEMNON Now, I will tell you what I want you to do, Clytemnestra.

CLYTEMNESTRA What is it? You can rely on me.

AGAMEMNON Well, firstly there is something I should do alone...

CLYTEMNESTRA What am I, her mother, to be excluded from?

AGAMEMNON I will give our daughter to the bridegroom in the presence of the armies.

CLYTEMNESTRA (*disappointed and irritated*) And what am I to do at that time?

AGAMEMNON Go back to Mycenae and look after our other daughters.

CLYTEMNESTRA What?! And leave my child?! Who is to hold up the wedding torch?!

AGAMEMNON I shall provide a light suitable for the couple.

CLYTEMNESTRA That is not the custom: we must not be disrespectful.

AGAMEMNON But it would be improper for you to mix with the troops.

CLYTEMNESTRA I bore my children and it is appropriate that I give them away in marriage!

AGAMEMNON It is appropriate that our other daughters are not left alone at home.

CLYTEMNESTRA I have left them well guarded.

AGAMEMNON Do as I say!

CLYTEMNESTRA By our Goddess of Mycenae: you see to your foreign ventures, but I should be the one to prepare the home and our daughter's marriages.

(*Exeunt* Clytemnestra, *and* Attendant(s) *with Orestes, abruptly and indignantly along the path to their lodgings.*)

AGAMEMNON My efforts are wasted; my hopes of getting my wife well away from here are dashed. I scheme and plan against those who are dearest to me – and I am defeated on every front.

47

Nevertheless, I will go with the priest, Calchas, to find out the will of Artemis, even though it bodes ill for me and for Greece.

Menelaüs teaches us a lesson: a man should either marry a good and loyal wife – or not marry at all.

(*Exit* Agamemnon *along the path to the camp*)

THIRD CHORAL SONG

[751]
CHORUS   *[strophe]*
    The white-foamed river Simoïs
    that torrents from the mountain side
    will see the gathering of the Greeks,
    the armies, ships and weapon's blaze
    against the lofty walls of Troy,
    that Lord Apollo holds so dear.
    I hear Cassandra, Priam's child,
    demented raves, and rips and tears
    her golden hair and bay leaf crown,
    the truth foretells, ignored by all:
    a deadly bane, Apollo's curse.

                               [antistrophe]

    The Trojans on their walls shall stand,
    atop the city's citadel,
    to face the bronze-clad God of War,
    whose high-sterned ships remorselessly
    by straining oarsmen driven on,
    from Simoïs' channels make their threat:
    they're here to seize the Helen fair,
    the sister of the Heavenly Twins,
    by force of arms to take her back
    to Greece, to Menelaüs' home,
    and Priam's Troy reduce to flames.

                                    [epode]

    The stone-built walls of Ilium's Troy,
    the city set in the Phrygian plain,
    will Ares, God of War, besiege,
    encircle it with severed heads.
    He'll crush the city, stone from stone,
    and it to blazing ruin raze.
    The wife and daughters of the King
    he will condemn to weep and mourn;
    and Helen, though she's born of Zeus,

will rue the day that she renounced
her lawful husband, broke her vows.
May that foreboding never rise
in me or in my children's minds
that grips the women of golden wealth,
of men of the Phrygian race the wives,
who sit and work yet at their looms
and ask each other nervously
"Who comes to drag me by my hair,
to make my tears defile my cheeks,
to pluck me from my homeland dear?"
It's you they want, yes, Helen, you,
the child whom swan-loved Leda bore:
  if true that Leda chanced
  to mate with Zeus, disguised,
  appearing as a swan;
  or else the Muses' songs
  are out of season, fail.

THIRD EPISODE

(*Enter* Achilles *along the path from the camp*)

[801]
ACHILLES Where is Agamemnon, our general? Will one of his
men tell him that Achilles, son of Peleus, wishes to speak
with him?
(*aside*) This wait at Aulis affects us all in unequal
measure. Some of us are unmarried who have left our
lands untended as we sit idly by here by the beach, but
others have also left wives and children at home, so
incredible is the enthusiasm that the gods have inspired in
us all to be part of this expedition.
But matters have now reached a head and I need to discuss
with Agememnon the problems I face: – and others, I
know, face problems of their own.
I have left my land and my father Peleus at Pharsalus. And
now I sit and wait here amidst the faintest of breezes
across the Euripus, and am left to keep my Myrmidon
army in check. But my men are becoming restless and say
to me:
"Achilles, what are we waiting for? How much more time
must we waste before we can start out for Troy?"
And then they say:
"Either act positively, if you are going to, or lead the army
home – Agamemnon and Menelaüs have delayed
enough."

(*Enter* Clytemnestra *along the path from her lodgings*)

CLYTEMNESTRA Achilles, I heard what you were saying and
have come out to speak with you.
ACHILLES Madam, I have the misfortune not to know you.
CLYTEMNESTRA Of course; we have not yet met. But I thank
you for your courtesy.

51

ACHILLES May I ask who you are? Why have you, a lady, come amongst the Greek warriors armed with their shields and spears?

CLYTEMNESTRA I am Clytemnestra, daughter of Leda and my husband is King Agamemnon.

ACHILLES I am most pleased to meet you; but it ill-befits a soldier to stand talking with a woman. (*turns to leave*)

CLYTEMNESTRA Wait; why are you running off? (*proffers her hand*) Take my hand as a happy beginning to your marriage!

ACHILLES What do you say?! Take your hand? Agamemnon would rightly disapprove.

CLYTEMNESTRA Disapprove? Of course, Achilles, you must take the hand of the lady whose daughter you are about to marry!

ACHILLES Marry your daughter? You leave me speechless, madam, except to say that your inventive mind has the better of you.

CLYTEMNESTRA I understand: young men are often bashful when they meet their prospective mother-in-law and talk of marriage.

ACHILLES But I have made no proposal to your daughter, madam; nor has Agamemnon discussed a marriage with me.

CLYTEMNESTRA What?! If you are surprised at my words, then I am astounded at yours!

ACHILLES Then be astounded. We can both only guess at what has happened. We are clearly both parties to a misunderstanding.

CLYTEMNESTRA This is awful! I am here to celebrate a non-existent marriage, so it seems. I am extremely embarrassed.

ACHILLES Perhaps someone has set out to mock the pair of us. Pay no attention to it – it is of no importance.

CLYTEMNESTRA Good day then. I feel considerably embarrassed. But also, I feel I have been wronged.

ACHILLES And good day to you. I will continue my search for your husband.

(*Agamemnon's tent door opens slightly: the* Old man *speaks from within*)

OLD MAN Achilles wait! I have something to say to you – and to you, lady Clytemnestra.
ACHILLES Who is that opening the door? You sound frightened!
OLD MAN A poor slave! I'm not proud of the fact: it's just how it is.
ACHILLES Whose? You're certainly not one of mine. You must be with Agamemnon.
OLD MAN I serve here (*indicating Agamemnon's tent*). I used to be in the service of this lady's father, Tyndareüs.
ACHILLES Well, state your business.
OLD MAN Is anyone else around?
ACHILLES We are alone – you can come out.

(*Enter* Old Man)

OLD MAN May good fortune and my own foresight save those dear to me!
ACHILLES Let us hope so.
CLYTEMNESTRA Let us not stand on ceremony, if you have something to say.
OLD MAN (*to Clytemnestra*) Do you recognize me? – who used to be faithful to your family.
CLYTEMNESTRA Yes, you used to serve my family.
OLD MAN And that Agamemnon received you as part of your dowry.
CLYTEMNESTRA Yes; you came with me to Mycenae and have been with us ever since.
OLD MAN I am well-disposed to you – less so to your husband.
CLYTEMNESTRA What have you to say?
OLD MAN Your daughter's father…with his own hand …intends to kill her.

53

CLYTEMNESTRA What?! Spit out what you have to say! You are making no sense!

OLD MAN He will slit her white throat with a sword!

CLYTEMNESTRA But…, is my husband sane?

OLD MAN He has a perfectly clear mind, except in regards to you and your daughter!

CLYTEMNESTRA Why?! What avenging spirit drives him on?!

OLD MAN Divine commands, interpreted by the priest Calchas. The sacrifice is ordered, to allow the armies to get under way.

CLYTEMNESTRA The end for me – and for her whom her father is to kill!

OLD MAN All so that Menelaüs can recover Helen.

CLYTEMNESTRA So Iphigenia is fated to die for Helen's return?

OLD MAN Yes. Her father intends to sacrifice her to Artemis.

CLYTEMNESTRA And talk of marriage was a mere pretext to bring us here?

OLD MAN Yes; he wanted you to be pleased to bring her here, to be married to Achilles.

CLYTEMNESTRA My daughter! You have come here to your death: you, and your mother as well!

OLD MAN Try to be calm.

CLYTEMNESTRA I must dry my tears.

OLD MAN How can you not weep for the loss of a child?

CLYTEMNESTRA How do you know all this?

OLD MAN I set out to bring you a letter, which overrode the earlier one you received…

CLYTEMNESTRA …telling me to bring or not to bring my poor daughter here?

OLD MAN …and told you not to bring your daughter here. Your husband had come to his senses.

CLYTEMNESTRA If you were bringing me the letter, why did you not give it to me?

OLD MAN Menelaüs found out and took the letter from me. He's to blame.

CLYTEMNESTRA Achilles, do you hear this?

(Achilles dismisses Old Man:
Exit Old Man *into Agamemnon's tent)*

ACHILLES You have been ill-used; I do not take my treatment
  lightly either.
CLYTEMNESTRA To think they kill my daughter with the
  promise of a marriage!
ACHILLES I blame your husband. This matter will not rest.
CLYTEMNESTRA *(falling to her knees before Achilles)* Though
  I am born of a god, yet I am not ashamed to kneel before
  you. What help is pride? Whom can I plead for, if not for
  my daughter?
  Help us, Achilles, in her and my misfortune. She was
  named your bride – falsely, I know – but named
  nonetheless. I even garlanded her for your wedding – but I
  am leading her to her slaughter.
  You will find yourself reproached if you do not help. Even
  though you are not marrying her, you have at least been
  named the husband of the wretched girl.
  In your mother's name, ('mother' – how can I say the
  word – a word that demands you defend me?) I have no
  altar to flee to – other than before your feet! No friend
  stands by me; and you have heard Agamemnon's
  monstrous plan.
  I have come, as you see, a woman to an army which is
  lawless and bold in its evil ventures across the seas. Your
  protective right arm is our only hope of safety.

CHORUS
  Our bearing children casts a powerful spell,
  of ceaseless struggling them all to protect.
[919]
ACHILLES My warlike nature knows no compromise: but I
  know distress in misfortune as well as due satisfaction in
  success.
  Such men as I have a reasonable hope of living our lives
  through properly and wisely; there is indeed a time to be

55

light-hearted and a time to concentrate one's noblest thoughts; and I, raised by godly Chiron, learnt a straightforward approach to life.

While ever Agamemnon and Menelaüs provide sound leadership, I will follow them. But I shall not, if their leadership is poor. In Troy, I shall be my own man and I shall honour the God of War with my spear as best I can.

Now you are suffering shamefully at the hands of those who are dearest to you. But I, so far as a young warrior can, will curtail your grief and banish it: never shall your daughter, named as my bride, die by her father's hand. I will not be entangled in your husband's web of deceit. My name, even though it wields no sword itself, has been enlisted to kill your daughter. The culprit is your husband: but I shall not escape the stain of guilt, if she dies because of me or marriage to me.

How she has suffered unbearably for a young girl! What dishonourable treatment she is enduring! And I would be the lowest of the Greek soldiers here, utterly worthless, the son not of great Peleus but of a vengeful demon – whilst Menelaüs would count as a man – if my name slaughters your daughter to benefit your husband.

By Nereus, father of my mother Thetis, King Agamemnon shall not touch your daughter – nor lay one finger on her dress. If he does, may barbarian cities flourish whilst my native Phthia dies.

Bitter will be the barley and sacred water sprinkled by Calchas to commence the sacrifice. What is a seer after all, but a man who occasionally chances upon the truth, but in the main talks nonsense?

I do not say any of this to secure a bride – there are countless girls eager for my hand – but because of the insolence, the *hubris*, of King Agamemnon towards me: he should have *asked* for the use of my name as bait. It was to *me* that Clytemnestra was persuaded to give her daughter in marriage.

I would have allowed it, if our journey to Troy depended on it. I would not refuse to help the common good of those with whom I campaign. But now I am treated with *contempt*: and I will lose *my* authority amongst *my* fellow commanders.

My sword will know whether someone has laid a hand on your daughter, if I defile it with blood before we reach Troy!

Be calm. I am no god, but I appeared as a mighty god to you. And so I shall prove.

CHORUS

How bravely does Achilles speak.
His mother, Thetis, would be proud!

CLYTEMNESTRA How can I give you proper praise? I neither want to tempt Fate by excess nor understate my thanks by deficiency. Good men like you hate gratitude too-profuse, and I am ashamed to intrude and dwell on my misfortunes. They are mine and you are unaffected.

But it is good that a noble man, with no personal interest, may help the unfortunate.

Pity us: our misfortunes deserve pity.

I first cherished an empty hope of your becoming my son-in-law, but now I fear that perhaps her death would be an ill omen for any future marriage of yours - which you would want to guard against.

But you spoke well from first to last. If you want it, my child shall be saved.

Do you want her to kneel as suppliant at your feet? I think it might be unbecoming, but if you want it, she will come with a free but modest eye. But if you will help us without this, let her remain dignified in her lodgings. But we must only allow her what we can.

ACHILLES Do not bring your child to me, lady: nor let us earn the reproaches of those who do not know the facts. An assembled army with few duties to perform loves idle and

57

malicious gossip. It will make no difference whether you approach me as suppliants or not. I have one great aim – to free you from your misfortune. One thing you must know – I shall not lie. If I lie or make an idle promise, may I die: but rather may I live to save the girl!

CLYTEMNESTRA May you be favoured by the gods for helping us in our distress.

ACHILLES Listen to what must be done now.

CLTEMNESTRA We will do whatever you say.

ACHILLES We must somehow persuade her father to come to his senses.

CLYTEMNESTRA But he has no resolve and goes in fear of the army.

ACHILLES We must argue and wrestle with his fears.

CLYTEMNESTRA My hope lies cold, but tell me what to do.

ACHILLES First of all, beg him not to kill the child. If he refuses, then you must come to me. If, however, he agrees, I need not interfere. You will be safe and I will remain on good terms with Agamemnon and will receive no blame from the army for having acted reasonably and without force.

CLYTEMNESTRA That is sensible and I will do as you say.
But if I do not succeed, where shall I see you again? In my distress, I need to be able to grasp the hand of you who help me in my troubles.

ACHILLES We will keep the necessary watch to ensure no-one observes you if you wish to pass in secret through the lines to me.
Do not let your family down. Tyndareüs does not deserve to be badly spoken of: he was a great man of Greece.

CLYTEMNESTRA That then is our plan: so be it. I am in your hands.
If the gods are watching, they will know you for a just and noble man. If they are not, what is the point of trying?

(*Exeunt* Clytemnestra *along the path to her lodgings, and* Achilles *along the path to the camp.*)

FOURTH CHORAL SONG

[1036]
CHORUS   *[strophe]*

What shout the God of Marriage raised,
as the Lybian flutes resounded wide,
when lyres, belovèd of the dance,
and clear-toned pipes their music made?
Across the slopes of Pelium
the Muses with their long-flown hair
and gold-strapped sandals came to sing
so lightly skipping o'er the ground
among the gods to the wedding rites,
and through the Centaurs' mountain sides
and woods they called the happy names
of hero Peleus and his bride,
the sea nymph Thetis, Nereus' child.
By Zeus's favourite, Ganymede,
from Phrygia come to serve the gods,
the overflowing deep red wine
in hollow golden cups was mixed.
And all along the glistening sand
old Nereus' fifty daughters danced
lithe sea nymphs, gaily round and round
in honour of the wedding day.

                                    [antistrophe]
Through forests, horse-borne Centaurs rode,
their heads all bound with green-leaved wreathes,
all eager for the revelry,
the sumptuous dinner, Bacchic wine.
They shouted loud "O Thetis, maid,
Apollo, through his Oracle,
foretells that you shall bear a son,
a blaze of light in Thessaly."
And Chiron sagely then proclaimed
"Your son shall lead the Myrmidons
with spear and shield to Priam's land

which he shall raze, reduce to flames;
he shall have donned the golden arms
and glinting high-plumed helmet proud
that in Hephaestus' forge were wrought,
as presents from his mother made,
from Thetis, who him soon shall bear".
And happily the gods made blest
this noble match, these marriage vows,
as Thetis, Nereus' daughter born,
that day the royal Peleus wed.

[Lament]
[1080]   *[epode]*
But as for you, the Greeks shall bind
your hair in wreathes about your head;
and, like a calf's that's undefiled
and led from deep and rocky caves,
your tender throat will soon be cut
and deathly deep red blood disgorge.
You were not raised 'mongst rustic pipes,
the whistling of the cowherdsmen,
but rather at your mother's side,
to wed a son of Inachus.
So where the face of Modesty,
and where the power of Virtue's arm?
Unholiness today holds sway,
and ancient Virtue, once held dear,
by men so disregarded is,
that Lawlessness o'ercomes the law.
And have we now no common goal
to avoid the anger of the gods?

CONCLUSION

(*Enter* Clytemnestra *along the path from her lodgings*)

[1098]
CLYTEMNESTRA (*aside*) I have come from my lodgings to watch out for my husband; he has left his tent and has been gone some time.

My poor child is in tears; I cannot bear to hear her cry her heart out. She has heard of the death her father is planning for her.

But here comes Agamemnon now. It will soon be clear to all what wicked intentions he has had for his own child.

(*Enter* Agamemnon *along the path from the camp*)

AGAMEMNON Clytemnestra, my finding you here gives me an opportunity to discuss certain matters with you – without our daughter being present – matters not suitable for girls about to be married to hear.

CLYTEMNESTRA What are these....matters?

AGAMEMNON Send the child out here to join her father; the sacred waters are ready, as are the barley to be cast on the purificatory fire and the calves to be slaughtered and offered to the Goddess Artemis before the wedding.

CLYTEMNESTRA You *speak* as if all is well: but I cannot commend your true intentions.

(*to Iphigenia offstage*) Come, daughter, out here. You know what your father intends. And, child, bring your baby brother Orestes with you.

(*Enter* Iphigenia *weeping, and* Attendant(s) *carrying the baby, along the path from their lodgings.*)

CLYTEMNESTRA (*to Agamemnon*) See, she is here at your order.

AGAMEMNON My child, why are you weeping? Are you not pleased to see me? Why are you so downcast?

CLYTEMNESTRA Why?! Why do you think?! Do you want a list?!

AGAMEMNON But what is wrong? You must agree, you both look equally distraught.

CLYTEMNESTRA Tell me truthfully what I ask, my husband.

AGAMEMNON You have no need to speak to me in that manner. You may ask me what you will.

CLYTEMNESTRA This child of yours, and *mine*, you intend to kill!

AGAMEMNON Ah!

You are speaking out of turn: Your suspicions are uncalled for.

CLYTEMNESTRA Calm down: but answer my question.

AGAMEMNON If you were to ask a sensible question, I would give you a sensible answer.

CLYTEMNESTRA I have no other question: and I want no other question answered.

AGAMEMNON O Gods of my Fate and Fortune...!

CLYTEMNESTRA ...and of our child and me. The same Gods of Fate and Fortune oppose the three of us.

AGAMEMNON In what way have you been wronged?

CLYTEMNESTRA You ask me that?! Are you out of your mind?!

AGAMEMNON (*aside*) I am destroyed: my secret is out!

CLYTEMNESTRA I can see your whole plan exactly. Your silence is confirmation: and your demeanour tells us everything. Do not trouble yourself to explain!

AGAMEMNON As you see, I am silent. Why add shamelessness to my misfortune by telling lies?

CLYTEMNESTRA Listen! I shall speak openly. We need no more pretence and riddles.

May I remind you in the first instance, that I married you against my will. You had killed Tantalus, my first husband and had taken me by force. I already had a child, whom you had snatched from my breast – and killed. My brothers, Castor and Polydeuces, the twin sons of Zeus, then war on you. You begged my aged father, Tyndareüs, to protect you – which he did, leaving you next to take me as a wife. Being married, I became reconciled to you, and you will testify that I have been a blameless wife to you and your family. Aphrodite knows I have been faithful to you and your home has been a joy to live in and a source of happiness when you have ventured abroad. Wives such as I are a rare catch. Shabbier women are not so rare.

I bore you a son and three daughters, one of whom, in your rashness, you are intent on taking from me. And if someone were to ask you your reason for killing her, tell me, what would you answer? Or would I have to speak on your behalf and say, "In order that Menelaüs may recover Helen"?

A fine price, I must say: to sacrifice one's own child in exchange for an evil woman – to buy what we most hate with what we hold most dear!

Suppose then that you depart on your campaign and leave me at home – and that you are away for a long time. How, in my heart, will I feel about you then? I shall look at the empty chair where she used to sit and at her empty bedroom and I shall sit alone with my tears and weep for her always: "He killed you, my child, – your own father. He killed you himself, with his own hand".

Now only the smallest pretext will be required for me and my surviving daughters to give you the reception you deserve when you do come home. By the gods, do not compel me to wrong you; but do no wrong yourself.

(*pausing to recover her composure*) What prayers will you offer as you sacrifice our child?

What benefit for yourself are you going to pray for as you slaughter her? – for shame on your return to match the disgrace of your departure?

And is it right that I pray for the gods to help you? Would we not be taking the gods for fools if we were to commend murderers to them?

When you return to Mycenae, will you embrace your children? You will have no right to. And which child will look you in the face, when you have taken one of them and killed her?

Have you given consideration to any of this? Or can you see no further than parading a sceptre and carrying on your military campaigns?

As a matter of fairness, you should say to your fellow leaders:

"Do you want, kings of Greece, to march against the land of Troy? Then draw lots for whose daughter is to die."

You would all then face equal risk, rather than have you pick out your daughter and present her to the army for slaughter. Or Menelaüs could kill his daughter Hermione, since the matter at issue is her mother Helen. As matters stand, I who have been faithful to you, am to be deprived of my daughter, whilst Helen, who has wronged her husband, will have her sweet young daughter to live with happily again in Sparta.

Tell me if I am being unfair. But if what I say rings true, see sense, spare my daughter, spare *your* daughter.

(*Agamemnon turns away from Clytemnestra, unable to answer.*)

CHORUS
We want our children safe from harm.
None, Agamemnon, disagrees.

(*Iphigenia slowly approaches Agamemnon and speaks after a pause*)

IPHIGENIA   Had I the eloquence of Orpheus, whose songs charmed the rocks to walk beside him and whose words cast a spell on anyone he chose, I would use that eloquence now. But as it is, my tears are my wisdom: I have nothing more. (*kneels at Agamemnon's feet*)

I fall a suppliant at your feet, with this body which your wife bore to you.

Do not kill me before my time. All mortals crave the light of day: do not condemn me to the underworld.

I was the first to call you father and the first you called your child. I was the first of your children to sit on your knee and to give and receive sweet kisses. As I grew, you used to say:

"My child, I shall see you happily married in the home of your husband, healthy and prosperous as befits my daughter." And I, holding on to your beard as now I take hold of your hand, would reply:

"And what about you, father? When you grow old, will I be able to welcome you into my home, and then be able to take care of you as you care for me now?"

I remember those times. You have forgotten them and are willing to kill me. Do not – by your grandfather and father, and by my mother here, who endured the pains of my birth and endures such pain again.

What have Paris and Helen to do with me? Father, why should they entail my death?

Look at me and give me a loving look, that as I die I will have this memory of you – if I fail to change your mind.

(*to baby Orestes*) My brother, you are too small to help, but weep with me; and in so doing, beg our father not to kill your sister. Even though you cannot speak, I sense you know my plight.

(*to Agamemnon*) Look: though silent, he begs you, father. Feel shame and pity: we both beg of you. He is young; I am older; by bringing our thoughts together, we must surely prevail!

To all men, the sweetest gifts are light and life: the world below is nothing. He is mad who prays for death; and even a poor life is better than a good death.

(*continues to weep*)

CHORUS
> O basest Helen, you the cause
> of strife for the sons of Atreus are!

AGAMEMNON I know what to pity and what not; and I love my children. I would be mad, otherwise. I understand the enormity of acting as I intend – and the consequences of failing so to act. I have no real alternative. You see the huge armies ready to sail: you see the kings of Greece in their bronze armour. They will never reach the towers of Troy nor raze the walls of that famous city, if I do not sacrifice you as Calchas tells me.

Some power of Aphrodite has driven the Greek armies mad with a passion to sail to a barbarian land to end the rape of the wives of Greece. They will kill my daughters who remain in Mycenae and you and me, if I disobey the command of the Goddess.

Menelaüs has not enslaved me, child, nor am I pursuing his aims. It is Greece to which I must sacrifice you, whether I am willing or not. As individuals, we are less important than the whole. Greece must be free; and you, child, and I must do what we can: and men who are Greek must not allow their marriages to be despoiled by barbarian force.

(*Exit* Agamemnon, *distraught, along the path to the camp.*)

[Sung lament]

[1276]
CLYTEMNESTRA
>O child, o strangers you,
>a father flees and yields you up
>to Hades dread and Death.

IPHIGENIA
>O Mother, my ill-fortune share.
>No longer will I see the day
>or sun's sweet light.

>In snow-driven groves of Phrygian Troy,
>on far Mount Ida's hillside steep,
>King Priam placed a tender babe,
>bereft of mother's care,
>abandoned to its fate of death.
>So Paris, you should not have lived,
>surviving green Mount Ida's slopes,
>as we are told,
>to herd your cows,
>beside the waters clear,
>the springs of woodland Nymphs,
>where meadows bloom
>with flowers fresh,
>and where goddesses pick
>the fragrant rose and hyacinth.
>Here, once, Pallas Athene came
>and Aphrodite, craftily,
>and Hera, wife of heavenly Zeus
>(the Cyprian nourishing desire,
>Athene with her spear,
>and Hera from her royal bed)
>in hateful strife
>their beauty to contest,
>and bring to me my death –
>and fame amongst the girls of Greece –

an off'ring made to Artemis.
My father, – mother, mother dear – ,
though I am wretched and alone,
will leave and me betray.
O Helen, what a bitter sight
you are to me, who am to die!
I perish, by unholy slaughter killed,
at my unholy father's hands!

Would that the bronze-beaked ships
had never come to moorings here
at Aulis, as they made
their voyage on to Troy,
and that great Zeus had never breathed
the adverse winds across the strait!
The gods to men blow varied winds:
of some they fill their joyous sails,
but grief to some they send
and others they becalm.
Hence, some set out, or ready make,
but others wait.
Beset with woes, beset with woes
is now the race of mortal men,
for whom ill-fate awaits.
What pain, o Helen, you have brought,
what suff'ring onto Greece!

CHORUS
    Oh we do sympathise with you,
    for what you never have deserved!

IPHIGENIA (*gripped by immediate fear*)
    Dear mother, see, a band of men come near…!
CLYTEMNESTRA (*calming*)
    …led by Achilles, whom you were to wed.
IPHIGENIA
    Ah! Let me go inside – I want to hide!

CLYTEMNESTRA
To hide?..
IPHIGENIA
...To see Achilles brings me shame.
CLYTEMNESTRA
What shame?..
IPHIGENIA
...from my ill-fated marriage vows.
CLYTEMNESTRA
Have no such pointless sensibilities,
or piety. Our needs demand you stay.

(*Enter* Achilles *along the path, accompanied by a band of his* Warriors)

ACHILLES
O Lady Clytemnestra...
CLYTEMNESTRA
...Please draw near.
ACHILLES
The armies make great clamour...
CLYTEMNESTRA
...on what grounds?
ACHILLES
...about your daughter...
CLYTEMNESTRA
...oh no, ill-omened words!
ACHILLES
They want her death...
CLYTEMNESTRA
...Does any speak against?
ACHILLES
I stood and faced the mob myself...
CLYTEMNESTRA
...and then?...
ACHILLES
...I faced a hail of stones...

CLYTEMNESTRA
      …you tried to help?
ACHILLES
    Indeed…
CLYTEMNESTRA
    …So then, who dared to threaten *you*?
ACHILLES
    They all dared…
CLYTEMNESTRA
      …But were your Myrmidons not there?
ACHILLES
    They were the first to threaten me…
CLYTEMNESTRA
      …We die!
ACHILLES
    They taunted me my wedding…
CLYTEMNESTRA
      …Your reply?
ACHILLES
    …They must not kill a future bride of mine ….
CLYTEMNESTRA
      ….Yes,
ACHILLES
    …whom Agamemnon named…
CLYTEMNESTRA
      …He sent for her.
ACHILLES
    Then I was shouted down with scorn…
CLYTEMNESTRA
      …Oh no!..
ACHILLES
    …but shall defend you still…
CLYTEMNESTRA
      …alone, 'gainst all?..
ACHILLES
    You see my warriors here...

CLYTEMNESTRA
...I pray success!
ACHILLES
...I shall succeed!...
CLYTEMNESTRA
...There'll be no sacrifice?
ACHILLES
No, none!..
CLYTEMNESTRA
...Will any come to take my child?
ACHILLES
Oh, many thousands – by Odysseus led.
CLYTEMNESTRA
...his own idea, or by the army sent?
ACHILLES
Commanded willingly...
CLYTEMNESTRA
...impious he!
ACHILLES
I'll hold her....
CLYTEMNESTRA
...Will he seize her nonetheless?
ACHILLES
...by the hair, no doubt...
CLYTEMNESTRA
...What can I do?
ACHILLES
Keep hold as well...
CLYTEMNESTRA
...Do not let her be slain!
ACHILLES
There'll be a *fight*!..
IPHIGENIA
...O Mother, hear me now!
[1369]
You must listen to what I have to say.

71

I see you wasting your anger on your husband: it is not easy to fight against the impossible. Rather, you should thank this man (*indicating Achilles*), till now unknown to us, for his eagerness to protect us.

But we must ensure that he is not open to further taunts from the armies: that would achieve nothing for us, whilst causing him great harm.

These are my thoughts then, mother.

Firstly, I am resolved to die. It would be a noble deed, devoid of selfishness.

Think it through with me.

It is to me that the whole of mighty Greece now looks. On me depend the sailing of our ships, the sacking of Troy, an end to barbarian raids on happy Greece and the seizure of her women. The barbarians will pay with their lives for Paris' abduction of Helen.

My death will secure all this and I will have fame, blessed by the gods, as the liberator of Greece.

Nor should you have too strong a desire for me to live: you bore me not as your child alone, but as a child of the whole of Greece. Countless men are ready with their shields, countless others sit at their oars; their fatherland has been wronged, but they are ready to fight the enemy and die for Greece. Is my one life to stand in their way? Is there any argument against what I say?

And there is a second reason. This man (*indicating Achilles*) must not be allowed to take on the entire Greek army – and to die – for the sake of a woman. Greece needs one man like him more than any number of women.

And if Artemis wants me as a sacrifice, am I, a mere mortal, going to prevent her, a goddess? To try would be futile. I give this body of mine to Greece. Sacrifice me! And sack Troy! That will be my everlasting memorial, my marriage, my children, my fame! It is right that Greece rule the barbarian, but not, mother, that the barbarian rules Greece! They are slaves; we are free!

CHORUS
So nobly spoken; But at fault
must be the realm of Fate and Gods!

ACHILLES Daughter of Agamemnon, some god would intend to make me happy indeed if I were to win your hand in marriage! I envy Greece for winning you, and I admire you for your love of Greece! You spoke well and worthily of your country. You are right not to fight the gods, who are too strong for you, but to think of nobility and necessity.
Now that I realise how worthy is your nature, I desire marriage to you all the more. See here: I would like to show kindness to you and take you to my home. And, by my mother Thetis, I shall grieve if I do not do battle with the Greeks and save you. Gaze at Death and see what a terrible thing it is!

IPHIGENIA Helen, through her beauty, will cause battles and death enough. But you, dear stranger, do not die for me nor kill anyone here. Rather allow me to save Greece if I can.

ACHILLES A fine sentiment, against which I can say nothing if you are so decided. Who could deny the nobility of your aim?
You might, however, still change your mind and you should know what I intend now. I shall go and put my arms near to the altar, not to allow but to prevent your death. You may have need of my promise when you see the blade approach your throat: I will not allow you to die through lack of preparedness.
I am going now, with my arms, to the temple of the Goddess and I shall await the outcome of events there.

(*Exeunt* Achilles *and* Warriors *along the path to the camp*)

IPHIGENIA
Why silence, Mother; why your tearful eyes?

73

CLYTEMNESTRA

My thoughts are cause enough to be distressed.

IPHIGENIA

Please cease; you'll me a coward make; now hear:

CLYTEMNESTRA

Do speak; no harm will come to you from me.

IPHIGENIA

Cut not your hair nor wear black clothes to mourn.

CLYTEMNESTRA

What say you now? My child, I'm losing you.

IPHIGENIA

But I am saved and you will win renown.

CLYTEMNESTRA

For your poor soul I still will need to grieve.

IPHIGENIA

No grief for me since I will have no tomb.

CLYTEMNESTRA

Your death for me will be sufficient tomb.

IPHIGENIA

Let Artemis' altar my memorial be.

CLYTEMNESTRA

My child, such noble words; how well you speak.

IPHIGENIA

I have the honour blest of serving Greece.

CLYTEMNESTRA

Yet how shall I of this your sisters tell?

IPHIGENIA

Do not about them wrap black mourning clothes.

CLYTEMNESTRA

But may I say to them kind words from you?

IPHIGENIA

Farewell – and Orestes raise to be a man.

CLYTEMNESTRA

So hold him close and see him one last time.

IPHIGENIA (*taking hold of baby Orestes*)

O dearest one, you've helped me all you can.

CLYTEMNESTRA
 What else, for your sake, can I do at home?
IPHIGENIA
 Do not my father, and your husband, hate.
CLYTEMNESTRA
 He'll face the consequences of his deeds.
IPHIGENIA
 Unwillingly he kills me...: Greece demands.
CLYTEMNESTRA
 ...by guile unworthy of his father's line.
IPHIGENIA
 But who will lead me out to the sacrifice?
CLYTEMNESTRA
 Oh, I must with you go....
IPHIGENIA
 ...No, no, not you!
CLYTEMNESTRA
 Your clothes I'll cling to.....

(*Enter a band of* Agamemnon's men)

IPHIGENIA
 ...Mother, hear my words:
 Stay here: it's better so for me – and you.
 (*she hands Orestes back to an Attendant*)
 Let one of these, my father's men,
 guide me to the grove of Artemis
 where I may serve as sacrifice.

CLYTEMNESTRA
 My child, do you go...?
IPHIGENIA
 ....not ever to return...
CLYTEMNESTRA
 ....to leave your mother...
IPHIGENIA
 ....wrongly, as you see.

CLYTEMNESTRA
>But wait and leave me not!..
IPHIGENIA
>>...You must not cry!

(*to the Chorus*) You women, sing the hymn of my doom to Artemis, daughter of Zeus.

Let the command go out to the Greek armies to observe an auspicious silence. Let someone bring out the sacrificial baskets and light the fire for the barley sprinkled in purification. Let my father, circle the altar keeping it to his right.

I come, keeping the Greeks safe in the knowledge of victory.

[Sung lament]
[1475]

>So lead me on – say I destroyed
>the Phrygian walls of lofty Troy!
>O bring me wreathes to cast about
>and garlands (here a lock of hair)!
>And sprinkle holy waters round!
>And wield before the altar dread,
>before the altar of Artemis,
>the mighty Goddess Artemis,
>the knife of sacrifice,
>so that my blood shall wash away
>the Goddess's demands!
>O Mother, Mother dear,
>I have no tears for you.
>To weep befits not sacrifice!
>You, you young women all
>across the sea from Chalcis come,
>together sing to Artemis,
>here, where the wooden ships,
>on my account becalmed,
>in the narrow straits at Aulis wait.

My land, my Mother Greece,
my Mycenean home...
CHORUS
(...the mighty city Perseus built,
for Cyclopean splendour famed...)
IPHIGENIA
...I, raised as beacon bright to Greece,
do not refuse to die!
CHORUS
Renown be yours and never fade!
IPHIGENIA
Bright lamp of day and light of Zeus,
a different time and fate awaits.
Farewell to you I say.

(*Exit* Iphigenia *and* Agamemnon's men *along the path to the camp.*)

[Lament continued]

[1510]
CHORUS
She goes, a girl, the bane of Troy
and of the Trojan race,
her forehead wreathed with flowers bright,
and sprinkled soon with drops
of consecrated water pure.
The altar grim of the Goddess harsh
with sacrificial blood will run.
The Greeks are all intent on Troy,
so let us raise our hymn,
as help we seek,
to Artemis, the daughter of Zeus:
"Accept our offering, Artemis;
and send our armies on to Troy
to overcome its perfidy.
To Agamemnon grant success,

undying glory, crowns and fame."

(*Enter* Second Messenger)

[1532]
MESSENGER Clytemnestra! Clytemnestra! Where is she? She must come out to hear what I have to say!

CLYTEMNESTRA I am here. What has happened? I cannot bear any more, but tell me the worst.

MESSENGER Your child: – I have a strange and amazing account to tell of her.

CLYTEMNESTRA Tell me as quickly as you can.

MESSENGER I will tell you all that happened – from the beginning – unless my mind – which is in a state of confusion – causes me to stumble.

So, then, when we came to the grove of Artemis and the fields around it where the armies were gathered, your child was led forward. The men immediately crowded round her; but as soon as Agamemnon saw her – coming to her death – he groaned deeply and turned away his face, covering his head to hide the tears which streamed from his eyes.

But she stood by her father and said:

"Father, I am here for you. I give my body willingly to those who lead me to the altar of the Goddess, to be sacrificed for my fatherland and for the whole of Greece, if that is what the Goddess requires. May you be proud of me; may your spear bring victory and may you return home safely.

"Let no Greek hand be laid on me now; for I meekly make ready my throat with good heart."

That is what she said. And everyone who heard, stood amazed at the virtue and bravery of this young maiden.

Then Talthybius, the herald, stood up in their midst, as was his duty, and ordered the army to be silent and to utter no inauspicious word.

And Calchas, the priest, drew his sharp sword from its sheath and placed it in a basket of beaten gold and placed a wreath on the young girl's head.

Then Achilles, taking the basket and the holy water, ran round the altar of the Goddess and said:

"Artemis, daughter of Zeus, slayer of wild beasts, bringer of day after night, accept this sacrifice of pure blood from a beautiful maiden's throat, offered by the Greek armies and by King Agamemnon, and grant a safe journey for our ships and the destruction of Troy's towers with our spears."

Agamemnon and Menelaüs stood looking down at the ground, as did all the men of the assembled armies.

Then the priest, taking hold of the sword and offering up a prayer, looked at the maiden's throat, to see exactly where to strike.

My mind was numbed with pain as I stood with head bowed.

And then – a sudden miracle!

The sound of the blow was clearly heard by all: but where the girl disappeared to, no-one saw.

The priest cried out and the armies echoed his cry – as they saw the unhoped for intervention of some god – hard to credit by those not there. A deer lay gasping on the ground: it was huge and beautiful to see. The altar was completely covered with its sprinkled blood.

You can imagine the happy voice of Calchas when he proclaimed:

"Leaders of all the Greek armies, do you see this offering of a mountain deer, which the Goddess has placed on her own altar? Artemis has preferred this sacrifice to that of the girl, so as not to defile her altar with noble blood. The Goddess is appeased, and will grant us fair voyage for our attack on Troy. Therefore, let every man take heart and go to his ship. We must leave the bay of Aulis today and set sail across the Aegean Sea."

When the sacrificed deer had been consumed in the
blazing flame of Hephaestus, final prayers were offered
for the safe return of the expedition.

Agamemnon sent me to tell you all this, what fate the
gods have granted him and what undying renown he has
earned throughout Greece.

I was an eye-witness – clearly, your child has flown away
to the gods.

Set aside you grief and your anger towards your husband:
the gods treat mankind in unexpected ways and keep safe
those whom they love. This day has seen your daughter
die and live again!

CHORUS
How pleased we are at this account!
He says your child lives with the gods!

CLYTEMNESTRA (*still heart-broken*) My child! Which of the
gods has stolen you? How can I speak to you? How can I
think that what I have heard is anything but nonsense
designed in vain to ease my sad grief!

CHORUS
But look you, Agamemnon comes.
He clearly wants to speak with you.

(*Enter* Agamemnon *along the path from the camp*)

AGAMEMNON My wife, our daughter has been a blessing to us!
And now she has true communion with the gods!
You must now take your young baby and start for home:
the armies are looking to set sail.
Farewell and be of good cheer! It will be some time before
I speak to you again on my return from Troy. May all go
well with you.

(*Exit* Agamemnon *along the path to the camp*)

CHORUS
>Farewell now, Agamemnon. Go!
>Success at Troy and safe return,
>enriched by all her finest spoils!

(*Exit* Chorus *along the path away from the camp.*
Then, exit Clytemnestra *distraught and angry, accompanied by*
Attendant(s) *along the path to their lodgings.*)

www.ingramcontent.com/pod-product-compliance
Lightning Source LLC
Chambersburg PA
CBHW070302290526